Machines At Work
Byron Barton

Copyright © 1987 by Byron Barton
Manufactured in China. All rights reserved.

For information address HarperCollins Children's
Books, a division of HarperCollins Publishers,
195 Broadway, New York, NY 10007.

Library of Congress Cataloging-in-Publication Data
Barton, Byron.
Machines at work.

Summary: During a busy day at the construction site,
the workers use a variety of machines to knock down
a building and begin constructing a new one.
[1. Building—Fiction.   2. Construction equipment—Fiction.
3. Machinery—Fiction.]   I. Title.
PZ7.B2848Mac 1987   [E]   86-24221
ISBN 0-694-00190-2.—ISBN 0-690-04573-5 (lib. bdg.)

17 18 19 20 SCP 30 29 28 27 26 25 24 23 22

HarperCollinsPublishers

H y, you guys!

Let's get to work

Knock down that building

Bulldoz that tre .

Dig up that road.

Load that truck.

Dump that rubble.

Now let's eat lunch

Next, dig a hole

Mix the cement

Lift that beam.

Build that building.

Build that road.

O.K. Stop the machines.

Let's go home.

More work tomorrow.